Enabling Trade in the Era of Information Technologies: Breaking Down Barriers to the Free Flow of Information

Summary

The transformative economic benefits of the Internet are under threat, as increasing numbers of governments move to impose onerous limits on information flow. The international community must take action to ensure the free flow of information online. Governments should honor existing international obligations including under the World Trade Organization (WTO) Agreement, prevent trade barriers created by information regulation, and develop new international rules that provide enhanced protection against these trade barriers of the 21st century.

To realize the full potential of the Internet as a global marketplace and platform for innovation, policymakers in the United States, the European Union, and elsewhere should pursue three steps to break down barriers to free trade and Internet commerce:

- Focus on and publicly highlight as unfair trade barriers those practices by governments that restrict or disrupt the flow of online information services.
- Take appropriate action where government restrictions on the free flow of online information violate international trade rules.
- Establish new international trade rules under bilateral, regional, and multilateral agreements that provide further assurances in favor of the free flow of information on the Internet.

This is an ambitious but achievable agenda. It offers opportunities for the U.S. government to better align the nation's trade priorities with the global economy and, in turn, create new jobs and export opportunities for the U.S. It can also provide concrete incentives for other governments to reduce or stop the restriction and disruption of information on the Internet.

Context
The need to protect the free flow of information online is more clear than ever. A confluence of trends has created a new international trade and business environment that calls for governments to ensure that the Internet remains open for global business.

The Internet has transformed traditional commerce, creating an astounding array of new economic opportunities and expanding international trade. More than three million Americans now owe their jobs to the Internet, and hundreds of thousands of businesses use the Internet to reach once-inaccessible international markets. This has had significant ripple effects throughout national and local economies, helping drive economic and job growth in the information age.

An open Internet has been and remains an absolutely critical component of the new information economy's ability to empower individuals and create shared information markets. Closed systems are antithetical to the Internet's success and will significantly disable its potential to support trade and innovation going forward.

But governments around the world are restricting, censoring, and disrupting the free flow of online information in record numbers. More than 40 governments now engage in broad-scale restriction of online information, a tenfold increase from just a decade ago. Today more governments are incorporating surveillance tools into their Internet infrastructure; blocking online services in their entirety; imposing new, secretive regulations; and requiring onerous licensing regimes that often discriminate against foreign companies. These actions unnecessarily restrict trade, and left unchecked, they will almost certainly get worse.

Taken together, these actions have created a very difficult international trade environment in which information platforms and services are impeded, businesses' revenue streams are undercut, access to information in key markets is disrupted, and discrimination against U.S. and other multinational businesses grows. Every day, evidence accumulates that governments must take concerted action to protect and promote the free flow of online information and Internet trade.

Section I of this paper demonstrates how the Internet has changed the global economy and had a positive impact on international trade. Section II describes both the range and common characteristics of government regulations and restrictions on information flow. Section III outlines the trade effects of these practices and describes the harm to economic and trade interests. Section IV and the technical appendix analyze how current trade rules can and should be used to contest trade-restrictive Internet barriers related to information flow. Section V lays out a negotiating agenda for the future and makes recommendations about new trade rules needed to address these barriers.

I. The Internet's impact on economic growth and trade

The past decade has clearly demonstrated the Internet's vital and ever-increasing role in generating global economic growth and international trade, and economists and technologists today regularly refer to the "Internet economy." The Internet has rightfully been labeled a "general purpose technology enabler" – a once-in-a-generation technological development that fundamentally changes how economic activity is organized and enables a productivity leap. It has "enable[d] the emergence of new business models, new processes, new inventions, new and improved goods and services and … increase[d] competitiveness and flexibility in the economy, for example by the increased diffusion of information at lower cost." According to the Organization for Economic Cooperation and Development, the Internet's impact on productivity may exceed the effect of any other technology enabler to date, including electricity and the combustion engine.[1]

The tremendous spread of the Internet – faster than the spread of any previous technology – has also created new, rapidly expanding markets. Online traffic has increased at a compound annual growth rate of 66 percent over the past five years.[2] Today more than one-quarter of the world's population (1.7 billion people) uses this technology to communicate, inform, create, and buy and sell across borders.[3] These 1.7 billion Internet users are a massive new consumer base for both Internet services like email and the hard goods and services that are increasingly advertised, marketed, or sold online.

Internet intermediaries, the "platform" companies that provide such services as search, commerce sites, and applications, represent a substantial and growing segment of developed economies. These businesses generally act as intermediaries between "upstream" services or goods being supplied, and users: e-commerce markets like eBay and Amazon that bring buyers and sellers together; search engines like Google and Bing that help users find resources on the web; "app stores" that allow computer programmers to sell their software products for particular devices; video or photo sharing sites like YouTube and Flickr where user-generated content is posted; social services like Twitter and Facebook that promote connections among Internet users; and many, many others -- including some that are likely to start up in a garage somewhere in the United States in the future.

These companies are major sources of employment and drivers of economic growth. In the United States, the Internet ad-supported industry has created more than 3 million jobs.[4] These firms range from familiar multinational companies to some 20,000 small businesses with fewer than 500 employees.[5] These industries contribute at least $300 billion to the U.S. GDP.[6] Annual Internet-

---

[1] Org. for Econ. Cooperation & Dev. [OECD], *Broadband and the Economy: Ministerial Background Report* 8-9, OECD Doc. DSTI/ICCP/IE(2007)3/FINAL (May 2007).

[2] Fed. Commc'ns Comm'n [FCC], *Connecting America: The National Broadband Plan* ch. 4 (2010).

[3] Miniwatts, Internet World Stats, *Internet World Users by Language: Top Ten Languages* (chart) (Sept. 30, 2009), http://www.internetworldstats.com/stats7.htm; Int'l Telecomm. Union [ITU], *The World in 2009: ICT Facts and Figures* 1 (2009), http://www.itu.int/ITU-D/ict/material/Telecom09_flyer.pdf. The total number of fixed broadband subscribers reached nearly 500 million by the end of 2009. *Id.* at 5.

[4]This figure does not include aspects of the Internet economy that are not ad-supported, so the number including those benefiting from this economy is much higher. Hamilton Consultants, *Economic Value of the Advertising Supported Internet Ecosystem* 24 (June 10, 2009).

[5] Hamilton Consultants, *Economic Value of the Advertising Supported Internet Ecosystem* 56 (June 10, 2009).

based commerce worldwide is expected to soon reach $1 trillion.[7] In the United States alone, online retail sales were over $132 billion in 2008.[8] Globally, Internet and telecom services contributed 3.3 percent of GDP in 2004, compared with 1.8 percent in 1990, with virtually every single economy enjoying growth in the sector.[9]

Given the borderless nature of the Internet, it should surprise no one that Internet firms have become important exporters in their own rights, as well as key generators of international trade. According to a study by Hamilton Consultants, large U.S. Internet corporations earn about one-half their revenues outside the United States.[10] In the case of Google, revenues from outside of the United States comprised 53 percent of total revenues in the first quarter of 2010, and more than half of Google searches come from outside the United States.[11]

Even in more traditional trade sectors, like the goods and services businesses, the Internet has also been transformative. The Internet has empowered businesses of all sizes to reach international markets in ways unimaginable a generation ago. It has dramatically reduced the high entry costs to export markets that has for centuries kept most small business limited to local geography. This transformation of industry happens in both the industrial and developing world. In the U.S. state of Georgia, a small manufacturing operation is reaching out to international customers through Internet advertising.[12] In Idaho, a wilderness tourism company has attracted international customers through online search ads.[13] And in the South American nation of Guyana, women are using online marketing to sell hand-woven hammocks to people around the world.[14]

Many companies rely on the Internet, including particular websites, as their key advertising platform. For instance, companies are projected to spend over $225 billion on Internet advertising over the next three years (2011-2013).[15] Google alone generated more than $54 billion in economic activity in the United States in 2009 based largely on returns that businesses received from advertisements run next to search results and on websites.[16]

---

[6] Hamilton Consultants, *Economic Value of the Advertising Supported Internet Ecosystem* 4 (June 10, 2009).

[7] Brian Hindley & Hosuk Lee-Makiyama, *Protectionism Online: Internet Censorship and International Trade Law* 3 (ECIPE, Working Paper No. 12/2009), *available at* http://ecipe.org/publications/ecipe-working-papers/protectionism-online-internet-censorship-and-international-trade-law.

[8] U.S. Census Bureau, *Estimated Quarterly U.S. Retail Sales (Adjusted): Total and E-commerce* (chart) (May 15, 2009), http://www.census.gov/mrts/www/data/html/09Q1table3.html.

[9] Int'l Telecomm. Union [ITU], *digital.life: ITU Internet Report 2006* 73 (2006), http://www.itu.int/osg/spu/publications/digitalife/docs/digital-life-web.pdf.

[10] Hamilton Consultants, *Economic Value of the Advertising Supported Internet Ecosystem* 7 (June 10, 2009). Note that the jobs measured by Hamilton Consultants are merely advertising supported jobs. As such, the number of jobs created by the broader advertising industry is higher.

[11] Google Investor Relations, *Google Announces First Quarter 2010 Financial Results* (Apr. 15, 2010), http://investor.google.com/earnings/2010/Q1_google_earnings.html.

[12] Google, *Google in Georgia*, in *Google's Economic Impact: United States 2009* (2009), *available at* http://www.google.com/economicimpact/pdf/google_economicimpact.pdf.

[13] Google, *Google in Idaho*, in *Google's Economic Impact: United States 2009* (2009), *available at* http://www.google.com/economicimpact/pdf/google_economicimpact.pdf.

[14] Simon Romero, *Weavers Go Dot-Com, and Elders Move In*, N.Y. Times, Mar. 28, 2000, *available at* http://www.nytimes.com/learning/teachers/featured_articles/20000330thursday.html.

[15] PriceWaterhouseCoopers, *Global Entertainment and Media Outlook 2009-2013* 30 (2009).

[16] Google, *Google's Economic Impact: United States 2009* (2009), *available at* http://www.google.com/economicimpact/pdf/google_economicimpact.pdf.

The Internet's impact on export growth is clear and demonstrable. According to one recent study, a 10 percent increase in a country's overall Internet penetration is associated with a 1.7 percent increase in export growth in the services sector. A lower, but similar correlation pertains to trade in goods.[17]

As a new dynamic and open force in the global economy, the Internet has helped produce phenomenal change and growth. This growth has been accompanied by increasing demand worldwide for information and services from beyond national borders. While many governments have welcomed the new trade, some have recoiled at the new openness – and are determined to restrict the flow of information across the Internet.

II. Government disruption of the free flow of information on the Internet

In the early years of the Internet, it was widely believed that government attempts to censor online communication would inevitably fail. President Clinton spoke of efforts by governments to block the Internet being like trying to nail Jell-O to the wall. Internet technologist John Gilmore observed that, "The Net interprets censorship as damage and routes around it."[18] But as time went on – and governments proved the optimists wrong – that utopianism subsided, replaced by a more realistic understanding of the promise and perils of the technology.

In less than a decade, as noted above, more than 40 governments have instituted broad-scale restrictions of information flow on the Internet. They have become both increasingly sophisticated and successful in controlling many aspects of the Internet and restricting information to varying degrees. They have moved from a more simplistic approach of denying access to more subtle techniques of controlling access, techniques that can be even more damaging than denial of access in the long run.[19]

Governments have pursued four basic strategies to controlling information on the Internet:
- Technical blocking of access to an entire Internet service (*e.g.*, a search engine, an online store, a platform for hosted content) or specific keywords, web pages, and domains.
- Licensing requirements or other means to force companies to remove search results, making it more difficult for users to locate particular content.
- Take-down requirements demanding the removal of certain websites, enforced by legal orders or by making whole domains invisible to users.
- Encouragement of self-censorship through means including surveillance and monitoring, threats of legal action and informal methods of intimidation.[20]

---

[17] Caroline Freund & Diana Weinhold, *The Internet and International Trade in Services*, 92 A.E.A. Papers & Proc. 236, 236 (2002); *see also* Caroline Freund & Diana Weinhold, *The Effect of the Internet on International Trade*, 62 J. Int'l Econ. 171, 172 (2004) (for trade in goods).

[18] Jack L. Goldsmith & Tim Wu, *Who Controls The Internet? Illusions of a Borderless World* 90 (2006).

[19] Ronald Deibert & Rafal Rohozinski, *Beyond Denial: Introducing Next-Generation Information Access Controls*, in *Access Controlled: The Shaping of Power, Rights, and Rule in Cyberspace* 4-7 (Ronald Deibert et al. eds., 2010).

[20] These four basic techniques were identified by the Open Net Initiative, a collaborative partnership of researchers at the University of Toronto, Harvard University, the University of Cambridge and Oxford University. See Open Net Initiative, *About Filtering*, http://opennet.net/about-filtering. Others use different taxonomies to describe the range of efforts to control information on the Internet. *See, e.g.*, Congressional-Executive Commission on China, *Hearing on Google and Internet Control in China: A Nexus Between Human Rights and Trade?* (Mar. 24, 2010) (statement of Rebecca MacKinnon, Visiting Fellow, Center for Information Technology Policy, Princeton University).

Most government control of Internet information consists of either direct government blockage of an Internet service, or regulation of the content they may carry. Direct government blockage of an Internet service is tantamount to a customs official stopping all goods from a particular company at the border. In other cases, governments demand that as a condition of providing service to a particular market, companies like Internet service providers and search engines block or disrupt services, websites, and content. In either situation, the result is a restriction on the ability of Internet companies to provide their services (and generate revenue accordingly), and a disruption in the trade of all other enterprises that use these services.

Some common characteristics of government restriction of the Internet include the following:

Opaque regulations that disrupt information flow

Governments in some countries impose requirements on online service providers without making these rules publicly available or establishing a legal process. Governments may make demands orally, threaten to revoke licenses or take other punitive action when informal orders are not heeded.

Some countries explicitly make it a crime for a service provider to reveal requests made by government authorities – even where there is no law enforcement or similar rationale for secrecy.

As two leading Harvard Internet scholars have concluded, "With the exception of a few places, no state seems to communicate much at all with the public about its process for blocking and unblocking content on the Internet."[21] The lack of transparency also enables governments to engage in other excesses as part of efforts to limit information. And it denies exporters an opportunity to seek redress, or even a way to discover what is being done to limit their access to this market.

Wholesale blocking of services

Governments or legal bodies regularly block in their entirety a range of information services including video sites, social networks and blogging platforms.

Turkey is a recent case in point. An individual public prosecutor in Ankara was able to block YouTube access for all Turkish users for over two years after YouTube rejected his demand that they remove a number of videos from the site globally because they were deemed to be breaching a Turkish law that protects the reputation of its founder Kemal Ataturk. An offer to restrict viewing for objectionable videos within Turkey was deemed inadequate by the Prosecutor - only the worldwide application of the Turkish law would have seen the ban reversed. Recently the videos at the heart of the ban were automatically removed as the result of a copyright claim. These were reinstated (though restricted based on IP address for Turkey) when the claim was not upheld. As a result, YouTube is newly accessible from Turkey but the power to ban it again in the same way remains until the law is clarified.

This service blocking is by no means limited to video platforms, but extends to all services that enable free flow of information to users in countries restricting this information. China

---

[21] Jonathan Zittrain & John Palfrey, *Internet Filtering: The Politics and Mechanics of Control*, in *Access Denied: The Practice and Policy of Global Internet Filtering* 36 (Ronald Deibert et al. eds., 2008).

has shut off Facebook, Flickr, and Twitter many times. Foursquare, one of the newest social networking services that has recently risen in popularity, was blocked in advance of June 4, 2010, in response to the number of users who set their location to Tiananmen Square as a way of paying their respects online.

The effect of such actions on trade and communications is often drastic, because it is usually the services most used by local users that are blocked by governments. Livejournal, a popular blogging service in many parts of Eastern Europe, has been intermittently blocked by the governments of Turkmenistan, Uzbezikstan, and Kazakhstan over the past two years. Another blogging service, WordPress, was blocked by Guatemala during a political crisis in June 2009. In the aftermath of the disputed Iranian elections, when citizens began sending out material unfavorable to the ruling regime, that government blocked Twitter, YouTube and Google's email service, Gmail. Google's blogging service has been blocked in multiple countries, as has its social networking site, Orkut.

Vietnam has blocked Facebook since last year, and is threatening to filter more sites in Internet cafes in Hanoi with a new regulation, to be fully effective in 2011. And Pakistan, Turkey, and Afghanistan have recently released court orders that allow the government to monitor and block sites like Google, Yahoo!, Amazon, MSN, Hotmail, and Bing for content considered "blasphemous" or anti-Islamic.

Bias against foreign competitors
In October 2007, Chinese officials – angry over the U.S. Congress award of its Gold Medal to the Dalai Lama and the opening of a YouTube domain in Taiwan – manipulated the so-called Great Firewall so that users who typed in web addresses for the three major U.S.-based Internet search engines (run by Google, Microsoft, and Yahoo!) were taken not to their site of choice but rather to the Chinese-owned search engine, Baidu.

Governments including China and Vietnam censor both services and content at international telecommunications network gateways, and subject Internet traffic coming from outside the country to special filtering regimes. This can result in degradation of services that do not originate within the country as authorities pick and choose what information foreign entities will be allowed to provide.

Arbitrary and capricious behavior
To make matters worse, governments sometimes apply laws and regulations haphazardly or maliciously. Officials in a number of countries have blocked or disrupted services because particular content offended their personal sensibilities or exposed personal improprieties, even when the content had no plausible connection to the government's objectives, or was available through other services as well. In other cases, there has been direct government intervention that has hurt both the reputation and sales of Internet firms.

In June 2009, government-controlled media in China singled out Google as a purveyor of pornography in order to justify the order that computer manufacturers install the so-called "Green Dam" software, technology that would allow the government to block users from seeing "harmful content." Although many Chinese-owned services and portals also carry pornography, the Chinese government shone its spotlight only on Google sites.[22]

The examples and anecdotes cited above are part of a larger trend that worries experts at the Open Net Initiative, Freedom House, Reporters Without Borders and other groups that track disruptions of online information flows. There is a growing consensus that governments must do more than appeal for the protection of human rights and encourage development of tools that allow users to bypass government firewalls. Censorship on the Internet poses a significant economic threat to companies seeking a level playing field as they establish markets overseas.

III. The impact of government restrictions on information in trade

Limitations on the free flow of information and restrictive Internet regulations are a clear threat to open markets and trade. Governments that limit or block the flow of information threaten not only the ability of companies to access and compete in their markets, but also threaten the very traits of the Internet that have made it into an engine of economic growth and put at risk the ability of the Internet-related business to continue expanding their exports, employment, and innovation.

Block the "ports" of 21st century trade

Internet filtering makes it harder for Internet companies to reach their customers, and it means that the businesses that rely on the Internet are likely to experience lower productivity.[23] According to an Australian government-commissioned study, experimental Internet filtering at the ISP level degraded network performance by between 2 percent and 87 percent, depending on the filtering software.[24] And when such filtering is applied only to foreign traffic, it means that foreign websites, and those businesses that rely on foreign websites to market and sell their products, become a second-best option to their local competitors.

The Internet is a 21st century trading route, and so when it is impeded, the commerce that passes through it is impeded too. A study that compared the role of the Internet and that of port facilities in trade facilitation, and found that the Internet is at least as important in facilitating trade: Improving the speed and affordability of Internet access could lead to a 4 percent increase in trade in manufactured goods, compared to a 2.8 percent increase associated with improving port efficiency.[25]

Hurt companies seeking to export their services to new markets

---

[22] Simon Elegant, *Chinese Government Attacks Google Over Internet Porn*, Time, June 22, 2009, *available at* http://www.time.com/time/world/article/0,8599,1906133,00.html; Wang Xing & Cui Xiaohuo, *Google "Used" in Online Porn Tiff*, China Daily, June 22, 2009, *available at* http://www.chinadaily.com.cn/china/2009-06/22/content_8306840.htm.

[23] Duncan Riley, *The Economic Cost of Internet Censorship in Australia*, Inquisitr, Feb. 5, 2009, *available at* http://www.inquisitr.com/17448/the-economic-cost-of-internet-censorship-in-australia.

[24] Australian Commc'ns & Media Auth., *Closed Environment Testing of ISP-Level Internet Content Filtering* 48 (2008). While the study predicted that "moderate to nearly nil performance degradation is possible," *id.* at 52, actual degradation depends on the technology used, and the study demonstrated substantial variance in the performance of different filters.

[25] United Nations Economic and Social Commission for Asia and the Pacific & Asian Development Bank, *Designing and Implementing Trade Facilitation in Asia and the Pacific* 85 (2009), *available at* http://www.unescap.org/publications/detail.asp?id=1352 (citing John S. Wilson et al., *Assessing the Potential Benefit of Trade Facilitation: A Global Perspective* 24-32 (World Bank, Policy Research Working Paper 3224, 2004)).

When a foreign government blocks or technically interferes with a website, it has either barred or undercut that business' access to the market. The Internet business cannot reliably offer its services, attract users to its site, or serve advertisements to Internet users in that country. The government action is the equivalent of shuttering the windows of a brick-and-mortar store, or, in the case of technical interference, stopping every third or fourth customer from entering the store. And the problems are particularly pronounced where a government interferes with a so-called Internet intermediary website, as it affects all of the business and individuals that use the site to communicate, trade, and advertise.

Consider the example where a government takes a website out of service for one week. For the intermediary company offering the service, that break will decrease revenue for the site by at least 2 percent on an annual basis.[26] For the company that uses the platform to advertise or sell goods and services, there will be a similar drop and a loss of trust in the platform. And given users' tendency to move to new services when the ones they use do not load quickly, let alone services that disappear for a week – the resulting perception of unreliability could result in both short- and long-term decreases in traffic.[27] In one study, over three-quarters of consumers said they would be less likely to return to a site that took too long to load.[28]

Beyond the impairment of speed and availability of sites, restrictive rules around the flow of information change the nature of the service that an Internet company can provide. The core business of intermediary companies is to provide access to the search results, hyper-links, websites, emails, blog entries, news, maps, calendars, spreadsheets, photos, and videos that drive interactions across the Internet; they are providing information and communication platforms. The utility of those services and the trust of users are both compromised when the product contains incomplete and distorted information.

Provide unfair advantage to local companies

When governments choose to manipulate the market in favor of local firms, it is naturally harder for foreign firms to compete. In China, for instance, numerous U.S. Internet services have been kept out or severely restricted, while Chinese versions of the same services have been permitted to operate; and in some cases, the Chinese sites contain their own share of "offensive" content. As an article in *Foreign Policy* noted:

> [I]n July 2009, after the riots...in Xinjiang, China blocked Facebook. Meanwhile direct Chinese copies of Facebook, Ren Ren Wang and Kai Xin Wang, have been enjoying enormous success. Also in the aftermath of the Xinjiang riots, microblogging site Twitter was cut off by the Chinese firewall for similarly dubious reasons. Less than two months later, Chinese Internet giant Sina launched a near identical microblogging service. ... Even a seemingly harmless site, like [Flickr], has been blocked in China, while its identical clone Bababian has grown steadily with foreign technology and no competition. Likewise, blog-hosting sites Blogger and WordPress have long been blocked in China. Instead Chinese

---

[26] Brian Hindley & Hosuk Lee-Makiyama, *Protectionism Online: Internet Censorship and International Trade Law* 6 (ECIPE, Working Paper No. 12/2009), *available at* http://ecipe.org/publications/ecipe-working-papers/protectionism-online-internet-censorship-and-international-trade-law.

[27] ShanShan Qi et al., *A Study of Information Richness and Downloading Time for Hotel Websites in Hong Kong*, in *Information and Communication Technologies in Tourism: 2008* 267, 268 (Peter O'Connor et al. eds. 2008) (citing C. Ranganathan & S. Ganaphy, *Key Dimensions of Business-to-Consumer Websites*, Info. & Mgmt., 39(6), 457-465 (2002)),

[28] JupiterResearch, *Retail Web Site Performance: Consumer Reaction to a Poor Online Shopping Experience* 5-7 (2006), *available at* http://www.akamai.com/dl/reports/Site_Abandonment_Final_Report.pdf.

netizens use Tianya, the 13th-most popular site in China. Far from being a sanitized land of boring blogs about daily activities ... [it] is a vitriolic, sensationalized, and hate-filled arena that makes Western gossip sites seem like the *Economist*.

Impede business operations
When governments impose non-transparent and arbitrary regulation on online services – as is often the case under restrictive information regimes – they make it difficult for businesses to execute commercial plans. To successfully export to or invest in a new market, a company needs to be able to understand the rules of the road and have some level of confidence that the government will not arbitrarily interfere with its business.

Hurt businesses that rely on the Internet to advertise or sell goods and services
Companies that sell or advertise goods and services on intermediary sites are severely impacted when the site is blocked or becomes unstable in a particular country: the small business that advertises on Google search through AdWords but does not reach certain markets because the search service is blocked; the artist and music publisher who do not reach a certain market because an entire online music store is blocked; the manufacturer selling its goods on an online marketplace like eBay that is blocked.

These restrictions on trade inordinately impact small businesses that only have the Internet as a means to reach a broad audience. For companies that are breaking into new markets, disruption of the services for even short periods of time can disrupt business plans and block their visibility to new customers at critical moments.

Hurt downstream businesses that cannot access services or goods
Businesses and consumers that rely on access to the Internet services are adversely impacted when these services are blocked or impeded as a result of Internet censorship. To take one example, the recent blockage of Google Docs in Turkey caused substantial disruptions for businesses that rely on that Internet service. Said one Turkish service provider: "We have created a Google document [page] and were running our operations from there; now we cannot communicate." As a result, they will be forced to migrate to more expensive platforms or applications that are not hampered by government restrictions.

Put the global Internet at risk
Restrictive Internet regulations have a broader negative effect on the shape and architecture of the Internet. The Internet was developed as an open network of networks: "The decision to make the Web an open system was necessary in order for it to be universal. You can't propose that something be a universal space and at the same time keep control of it."[29] This remains true today.

Governments that build censorship into networks change the architecture and nature of the Internet in ways that damage trade and innovation. As the Federal Communications Commission recently observed, "Today's Internet embodies a legacy of openness and transparency that has been critical

---

[29] World Wide Web Consortium (W3C), *Frequently Asked Questions*, http://www.w3.org/People/Berners-Lee/FAQ.html (quoting Sir Tim Berners-Lee, an engineer widely credited with creating the concept and protocols of the World Wide Web).

to the network's success as an engine for creativity, innovation, and economic growth;"[30] "[i]ts continued health and growth...depend on its continued openness."[31] This statement is true not only in the United States, but worldwide; any restrictions on the flow of information globally affect the Internet here.

Fragmenting the global Internet into "local" networks operating under different rules necessarily complicates and slows trade and economic growth. It makes information delivery uneven and re-creates the disparities among people's access to information that the Internet has heretofore succeeded in eliminating. A divided Internet impedes the ability of businesses to reach a global market and impedes the collaboration and network effects that create so much of the value for many Internet businesses and Internet users.

In sum, when Internet services are blocked or restricted, or the Internet is regulated in a non-transparent or arbitrary manner, the substantial economic and trade benefits of the Internet are put at risk. Trade officials and policymakers should be deeply concerned about the impact of Internet information restrictions on economic growth and trade interests. And, they should be ready to use current trade rules and negotiating forums to reduce this threat.

IV. How disrupting the free flow of information can violate international trade rules

Governments often pursue restrictions on accessibility of certain kinds of information in ways that directly hurt international trade and the international trading system. Governments in the United States, the EU and elsewhere have a variety of existing trade agreements – principally the WTO General Agreement on Trade in Services (GATS) – that can and should be applied where appropriate to combat restriction and disruption of information delivered by the Internet.[32] The GATS has been in place since 1995, and expands the WTO rules from trade in goods to trade in services, from financial services to telecommunications and computer services, including cloud and other Internet-based services. Indeed, decisions by the WTO Appellate Body in recent cases, especially in the case of China's regulation of the import of various media content, demonstrate that information restrictions are subject to GATS disciplines. The rules in GATS can and should be used to help constrain government behaviors limiting information flow.

The GATS imposes restrictions on the way that governments can regulate trade in services, a broad category including knowledge- or information-based trade. In particular, GATS requires WTO Members to:
- Be transparent about government actions affecting trade in services;
- Provide judicial or independent review of administrative decisions affecting trade in services;
- Reasonably, objectively, and impartially administer rules affecting trade in services;
- Provide non-discriminatory treatment, including treating foreign firms no less favorably than domestic firms;

---

[30] Fed. Commc'ns Comm'n [FCC], Notice of Proposed Rulemaking, *In the Matter of Preserving the Open Internet*, ¶ 17, FCC 09-93 (Oct. 22, 2009).

[31] Fed. Commc'ns Comm'n [FCC], *Connecting America: The National Broadband Plan* ch. 4 (2010).

[32] For a more in-depth discussion of the obligations of WTO Members under GATS, please see the Technical Appendix.

- Ensure that foreign service suppliers have reasonable and non-discriminatory access to public telecommunications networks, including to move information within and across borders; and
- Provide fair market access for services and service providers.

There are clearly exceptional cases when pledges of transparency, review, impartial administration, non-discrimination and market access will not be followed. But the WTO negotiators set clear limits on the ability of Members to invoke such exceptions. For example, a "public order" exception is only available in situations where a genuine and sufficiently serious threat is posed to one of the fundamental interests of society. And, in order to justify any derogation from the rules, governments must:

- Show that the measure is necessary to achieve a stated objective (that is not simply "public order" but rather a serious threat to society);
- Not have any "reasonably available" less restrictive alternative; and
- Apply the measure without prejudice.

It is now up to other Members to ensure that exceptions do not become the rule -- protecting Members' right to pursue legitimate policy goals while preventing the broad application of exceptions that would undermine the value of the GATS. Trade officials should continue to enforce international trade agreements, including the legal framework described in more detail in the Technical Appendix to this paper, to promote the free flow of information.

V. Toward a 21st century Internet trade agenda

As the Internet grows, Internet-related trade increases, and the global economy becomes more interconnected, governments in the United States, EU and elsewhere should be taking concrete steps to ensure that rules in the next generation of trade agreements reflect new challenges of Internet trade. In this new era, addressing the trade-related problems posed by government censorship and disruption of the Internet will be critical. Fresh, creative thinking will be required in order to properly address the unprecedented problems and opportunities that arise every day.

Two arenas deserve primary attention. First, governments must close gaps in the existing WTO framework in order to ensure that all GATS disciplines apply to all Internet trade. Second, governments must negotiate new rules that reflect today's information economy and include them in bilateral and multilateral trade agreements.

Coverage for all Internet services in trade agreements
Some GATS provisions – including national treatment and market access – apply only to services specifically listed by WTO Members in their schedules. While many countries used broad listings that would clearly expand to cover today's Internet services, others did not. This is not surprising, given that the Internet was in its infancy when most WTO schedules were negotiated.[33] But now

---

[33] Although the entire Internet, in its current form, is a primarily post-GATS development, the classification question is particularly relevant with respect to Internet intermediary services, which are a new set of services developed uniquely for the Internet environment. The concern is less present in the context of Internet transmissions per se (which is more

attention must be paid to closing these gaps so that schedules reflect the development to date – and make room for the continuing evolution – of the Internet and Internet-related services.

Governments like the United States, Canada, Japan, and the European Communities have made forward-looking proposals in the pending Doha Development Agenda round of WTO negotiations.[34] Covered under both the Computer and Related Services sector and the Telecommunications sector, these proposals would begin to rationalize and increase certainty to the scheduling of Internet services. These efforts deserve support, recognizing that the various proposals themselves – some of which are based on analytic frameworks that predate the start of the Doha Round – need to be updated and aligned to ensure they are comprehensive. Ultimately, a new round of commitments will be needed to ensure that all GATS disciplines apply to all of the economic activities on the Internet.

Beyond making the "positive list" of covered service sectors as broad as possible, governments should also advocate a "negative list" approach, which the United States uses in its free trade agreements, such that all service sectors are covered by national treatment, market access, and other disciplines unless a country specifically negotiates to *exclude* a particular sector. This approach avoids the problem of classifying new and emerging services that cross multiple sectors while maximizing ongoing trade liberalization.

Priorities for promoting Internet trade

In order to successfully reduce restrictions on and disruption of the Internet, governments must focus on three critical areas as they negotiate trade agreements: advancing the unrestricted flow of information; promoting new, stronger transparency rules; and ensuring that Internet services can be provided without a local investment.

Advancing the unrestricted flow of information

Information is the currency of the Internet and the innovation economy. The Internet's power and ability to deliver benefits, including to the international trading system, depends on the free flow of information across the entire global network. When data is blocked or disrupted, a wide range of businesses and consumers who depend on the Internet as a tool of trade are potentially affected.

Governments should therefore insist on trade agreements that explicitly recognize this and establish a presumption in favor of the free flow of electronic information. In some sense, this is simply applying the same concepts that have long been accepted in the realm of goods trade, and updating them to adapt to the 21st century economy.

Governments have long agreed that any restriction on the importation of goods should be prohibited[35]. In addition there is consensus that, to the extent that any technical regulations

---

clearly covered by the existing basic telecommunications service provider classification categories) and providers of other identified services who simply provide those services via the Internet (in which case governments have agreed that these services are covered by traditional service categories, regardless of the mode by which they are provided across borders).

[34] *See, e.g.,* Council for Trade in Services, Committee on Specific Commitments, *Communication from Albania, Australia, Canada, Chile, Colombia, Croatia, the European Communities, Hong Kong China, Japan, Mexico, Norway, Peru, the Separate Customs Territory of Taiwan Penghu, Kinmen and Matsu, Turkey, and the United States,* TN/S/W/60, S/CSC/W/51 (Jan. 26, 2007).

[35] GATT Article XI provides for the elimination of prohibitions or other quantitative restrictions on imported products.

are imposed that restrict trade, they should be limited to pursuit of legitimate governmental objectives and tailored to be no more trade restrictive than necessary to achieve that objective.[36] Other than tariffs, which have to be negotiated on a reciprocal basis, the default position under the WTO is that governments may not restrict imports of goods, and any deviations from that must be justified.

Trade officials should work to ensure that all governments accept the same presumption for the Internet – a presumption that governments may not restrict online information flows. While this concept can be translated into binding trade agreement language in different ways, the end result must put the burden on governments to justify with particularity any censorship or other disruption of the Internet. And in such scenarios, governments must tailor restrictions narrowly, spell out legitimate government objectives that are being advanced, and provide basic legal process to affected service providers.

The United States and Korea took an initial, positive step in this direction in 2007 by agreeing to the following provision in the Korea-U.S. Free Trade Agreement (KORUS):
> "Recognizing the importance of the free flow of information in facilitating trade, and acknowledging the importance of protecting personal information, the Parties shall endeavor to refrain from imposing or maintaining unnecessary barriers to electronic information flows across borders."[37]

This provision applies to any measure that disrupts information flows and applies to all digital content, whether goods or services.

The U.S. and other governments should improve the KORUS language and incorporate it into other trade agreements. Among other things, the provision should be revised to be binding – in KORUS it is an agreement to "endeavor to refrain from" certain restrictions – and it should apply to all electronic information flows, not just those "across borders".

One important opportunity to negotiate a similar rule is the newly launched Trans-Pacific Partnership Trade Agreement (TPP) – which the United States, Australia, Brunei Darussalam, Chile, New Zealand, Peru, Singapore, Vietnam, and Malaysia are now negotiating. This agreement includes a mix of developed and developing countries and also countries with different levels of transparency, process and openness when it comes to Internet regulation. As such, it is an ideal opportunity to establish broadly-applicable rules. It is also being negotiated in Asia, and as such will cover markets that represent key growth opportunities for U.S. Internet firms and the goods producers that depend on information flow to market internationally. Finally, it is the first Free Trade Agreement (FTA) that the Obama Administration is negotiating, and as such will make an important statement about U.S. trade priorities.

---

[36]Under the WTO regime governing trade in goods, Article 2.2 of the Agreement on Technical Barriers to Trade (TBT) provides that all "technical regulations" (i.e., those setting out mandatory product characteristics or related processes and production methods) affecting trade in goods must be the least trade restrictive measure that achieves a legitimate government objective.

[37] Korea-U.S. Free Trade Agreement [KORUS] art. 15.8 (Cross Border Information Flows), signed June 1, 2007, *available at* http://www.ustr.gov/trade-agreements/free-trade-agreements/korus-fta/final-text.

The European Union also has opportunities to advance the Internet trade agenda in its pending trade negotiations with India and Canada, as well as negotiations it is pursuing in Southeast Asia and elsewhere. Renewed partnership agreements negotiations with Russia might also offer the EU a particularly important opportunity.

The U.S. and other governments should further embed these principles in less comprehensive agreements, such as those reached under the Asia Pacific Economic Cooperation (APEC) forum or trade and investment framework agreements. APEC offers a particularly interesting opportunity because Japan and the United States, the current and next hosts for APEC forums, both recognize the importance of the Internet economy.

Finally, governments should be looking to reach agreement on these principles in the WTO. If the Doha Round moves forward and negotiations proceed on trade in services, free flow of information should be on the table. There are also opportunities at the WTO in the context of negotiations regarding new Members. Russia is in the final stages of its WTO accession negotiations, and various Middle Eastern countries are negotiating accession too. Many of these countries impose onerous restrictions on the Internet, so pursuing specific agreements in the context of their accessions makes sense.

Promoting new, stronger transparency rules

As noted above, transparency provides an important check against excessive and unfair censorship and disruption of the Internet, which is today largely and perennially opaque in many countries. In addition to better enforcing existing transparency and due process regimes, governments should go beyond current rules and commit to:

- Publish, on a regular schedule, all orders or requests made to providers of Internet information services to limit information provided on the Internet.
- Publish in advance and for public comment all measures that affect the provision of Internet information services.
- Publish the terms of all licenses (including ancillary documents that affect the terms of the license) for the provision of Internet information services to the extent a license is required.
- Advocate simultaneously for the elimination of licensing requirements for Internet services. As long as governments are permitted under international rules to require that business obtain licenses to provide various online services, the licensing process should be maximally transparent and open.
- Publish all decisions on licensing applications and all revocations, including the reasons for the decision or revocation with citation to relevant legal authority.

Ensuring that Internet services can be provided without a local investment

Governments often are able to succeed in abusive regulation of Internet companies and information because they require that data be stored in-country, effectively requiring local investment. Requirements like this reduce the economic efficiency of the Internet, which otherwise allow a business in any one country to easily reach users and consumers around the world.

Companies should be able to decide where to establish the data centers that are vital to their operations. A provider of information services might for its own reasons choose to establish a local affiliate and build/lease servers locally, such that when a user requests its services by entering a URL address in his or her web browser, that request is ultimately routed to a server in the same country. Alternatively, the company might choose to provide its service on a wholly "cross-border" basis, hosting all its data on central servers it maintains in one location globally or in a location outside the borders of the country to which the service is being provided. The user should experience the same convenient, intelligent and safe service.

From an international trade perspective, it ought to be the same – the provider of the particular service should be able to provide its service either on a cross-border basis or through a local investment and be assured of the same treatment.

While the GATS already establishes the framework to ensure the free flow of services across borders, it is not a generally-applicable requirement for all services; specifically, a Member must have listed the relevant Internet services on its WTO schedule and provided for no national treatment limitations. Governments should insist that these assurances – that Internet services can be supplied from any location and that governments cannot demand data be stored locally – be made explicit and embraced across the board in future trade agreements.

VI. Conclusion

Over the last two decades, the Internet has had transformational effects on productivity, job creation, access to new markets, and international trade. Today, this engine of economic growth is increasingly coming under attack by government policies that restrict the free flow of information online. These restrictions erect substantial barriers to international trade and threaten the open architecture that is the key to the Internet's economic and broader success.

Given the tremendous stakes involved, policymakers must develop and aggressively implement a proactive agenda that aligns Internet policy with the core principles of international trade. First, governments should not treat Internet policy and international trade as stand-alone silos, and recognize that many Internet censorship-related actions are unfair trade barriers. Second, governments should object to measures that affect information flow and that are insufficiently transparent, unreasonably administered, biased in favor of domestic players, or inconsistent with countries' WTO market access commitments, and consider appropriate trade actions. Third, governments should negotiate new trade disciplines that reflect the growing role of Internet-related trade in the global economy, to provide even stronger tools to combat measures that restrict information flow and the Internet.

These issues present not only a tremendous challenge, but an opportunity – an opportunity for public officials in the United States, European Union and elsewhere to align trade policy with the 21st century economy and to promote the many trade and other benefits that come from an open Internet.

Technical Appendix: Applicability of the WTO rules to restrictions on free flow of information

The following is a framework for how trade rules should be applied to information-restrictive regimes, not an explanation of how rules could be applied in a particular case. Whether a particular government's actions are consistent with its international trade commitments can only be judged on a case-by-case basis.

WTO General Agreement on Trade in Services (GATS) applies to information restrictions including censorship-related measures

By its own terms, the GATS "applies to measures by [WTO] Members *affecting trade in services*."[38] Whether the government law, regulation or other action is described as one of public order or public morals regulation is irrelevant to whether the GATS disciplines apply. As one WTO dispute settlement panel has put it, "no measures are excluded *a priori* from the scope of the GATS."[39]

The fact that information regulation and censorship-related measures fall under WTO authority has been illustrated clearly in a recent case that the United States brought against China regarding regulation of imports and distribution of publications and audiovisual products.[40] China sought to justify some of its restrictions – in that case, restrictions on foreign investment in import and distribution of books, movies, and other "culturally sensitive" content – on the basis that it was seeking to protect public morals and control content.

The United States did not challenge the level of censorship that China sought to achieve, but rather the *means* that China was using to pursue its objective. The decisions of the WTO panel and Appellate Body in that case demonstrate that a government's desire to control content on the Internet does not give it carte blanche to ignore WTO rules.[41]

Structure of the GATS

The GATS is organized into wo sets of obligations. One applies to all government regulation of trade in services, regardless of whether a WTO Member has made specific commitments to liberalize a particular service sector. The second applies only to those service sectors that the Member has listed on its WTO "schedule" of commitments.

Some of the WTO disciplines relevant to Internet information regulation – notably those regarding transparency – fall in the first category, and thus apply to all Members. Nearly every country in the world – exceptions include Iran, Russia, Syria, and Yemen – are WTO Members, giving these baseline provisions very wide applicability.

Other potentially relevant commitments – such as those pertaining to reasonable, objective, and impartial administration of laws, national treatment and market access – depend on whether the particular WTO Member includes relevant Internet services in its WTO list of commitments. On the one hand, because most schedules were drafted during the 1990s, when the Internet was in its

---

[38] GATS Art. I:1.
[39] Panel Report, *European Communities – Bananas*, ¶ 7.285, WT/DS27/R/USA, (May 22, 1997).
[40] Appellate Body Report, *China – Publications and Audiovisual Products*, WT/DS363/AB/R (Dec. 21, 2009); Panel Report, *China – Publications and Audiovisual Products*, WT/DS363/R (Aug. 12, 2009).
[41] *Ibid.*

infancy, commitments in this area are incomplete for most countries. On the other hand, many countries made commitments that encompass various Internet services (usually under the name of value-added telecom services, computer and related services, or audiovisual distribution services).

In fact, WTO dispute settlement panels have underscored the importance of "technological neutrality" in deciding how to construe a Member's trade commitments. In the *United States – Online Gambling* case, the panel noted that "GATS does not limit the various technologically possible means of delivery" of cross-border services.[42] And in the *China – Audiovisual* case, the Appellate Body opted for a wide interpretation of terms, dismissing the notion that GATS schedules should be interpreted based only on the meaning that particular terms had at the time negotiations were completed. In that case, it was found that the commitment for "distribution of audiovisual products" must extend to distribution of those products over the Internet, even if the distribution model had not been commercially offered at the time the commitment was made.[43]

To the extent that there are gaps in the GATS framework – for instance, that some Members have not listed particular sectors in their WTO schedules – Member governments should fill those gaps (see Section V). But where existing rules are relevant, they should be interpreted broadly and brought to bear as technology changes and new products and distribution platforms emerge.

Relevant GATS obligations
The GATS imposes broad restrictions on how governments may regulate trade in services, including how they administer rules and whether they provide fair access to their domestic markets. When governments impose obstacles that block information and harm trade, these international rules can be used to help constrain such behavior.

Six GATS obligations on WTO Members are particularly salient: (1) transparency; (2) provisions on independent review of administrative decisions; (3) reasonable, objective, and impartial administration of rules; (4) non-discrimination (including the right to provide services from one country to another without investing locally); (5) reasonable and non-discriminatory access to public telecommunications networks; and (6) market access.

1. <u>Ensure transparency.</u> As noted above, one of the most common features of regimes that restrict the flow of information on the Internet is their lack of transparency. Many governments do not even make publicly available their basic rules on restricting content while others hide obligations imposed on Internet intermediary businesses. This secrecy in regulation runs counter to a core tenet of the WTO: regulation that affects trade should be transparent, so that businesses can know the rules of the road and all parties have a chance to provide input. Transparency in regulation ultimately promotes accountability; as a provision that applies to all WTO Members, it should be leveraged to improve Internet information regulation globally.

   The WTO Appellate Body – its highest adjudicative body – has recognized the importance of Members' transparency obligations :

---

[42] Panel Report, *United States – Gambling Services*, ¶ 6.281, WT/DS285/R (Nov. 10, 2004).
[43] Appellate Body Report, *China – Publications and Audiovisual Products*, ¶¶ 396-397, WT/DS363/AB/R (Dec. 21, 2009). In that case, the panel had concluded that the electronic distribution service was available at the time China made its commitments, but did not rely on that point for its conclusion that electronic distribution was covered.

[The provision] may be seen to embody a principle of fundamental importance – that of promoting full disclosure of governmental acts affecting Members and private persons and enterprises, whether of domestic or foreign nationality. The relevant policy principle is widely known as the principle of transparency and has obvious due process dimensions. The essential implication is that Members and other persons affected, or likely to be affected, by governmental measures imposing restraints, requirements and other burdens, should have a reasonable opportunity to acquire authentic information about such measures and accordingly to protect and adjust their activities or alternatively to seek modification of such measures.[44]

In particular, GATS (Article III:1) requires governments to publish all laws, regulations, and other measures that apply generally and that pertain to or affect the operation of the GATS, in a prompt fashion but in any event (except in emergency situations) by the time of their entry into force. Where publication is not practicable, Members are required to find another way to ensure that Members and the public at large can access them.

WTO panels have rebuked governments for insufficient transparency under analogous provisions in the General Agreement on Tariffs and Trade (GATT, Article X). For instance, in 1998, when the United States failed to issue formal notices of denial for applications to be able to export shrimp, or state a basis for such denials, it was found to be acting contrary to WTO transparency and related provisions.[45]

2. Independent review of administrative provisions. In addition to transparency rules, the GATS also calls on Members to provide some measure of judicial or independent review of administrative decisions affecting trade in services. WTO Members with harsh rules on the flow of information tend to skirt this requirement. The particular GATS provision (Article VI:2(a)) is as follows:

> Each Member shall maintain or institute as soon as practicable judicial, arbitral or administrative tribunals or procedures which provide, at the request of an affected service supplier, for the prompt review of, and where justified, appropriate remedies for, administrative decisions affecting trade in services. Where such procedures are not independent of the agency entrusted with the administrative decision concerned, the Member shall ensure that the procedures in fact provide for an objective and impartial review.

While the GATS allows for exceptions based on a Member's constitutional structure or the nature of its legal system, it sets a baseline prohibition on unchecked administrative authority over trade in services.[46] Governments should use this

---

[44] Appellate Body Report, *United States – Restrictions in Imports of Cotton and Man-made Fibre Underwear*, WT/DS24/R, pp. 20-21 (Feb. 10, 1997) (construing the comparable transparency provisions, Article X, in the GATT 1994).

[45] Appellate Body Report, *United States – Import Prohibition of Certain Shrimp and Shrimp Products*, WT/DS58/AB/R, para. 183 (Oct. 12, 1998). *See also* Panel Report, *Dominican Republic – Cigarettes*, WT/DS302/R (May 19, 2005), paras. 7.395, 7.414

[46] *See* GATS art. VI:2(b) ("The provisions of subparagraph (a) shall not be construed to require a Member to institute such tribunals or procedures where this would be inconsistent with its constitutional structure or the nature of its legal system."). At the same time, some WTO Members made more specific commitments with respect to independent review in the context of their accession agreements. China committed as follows in its Protocol of Accession (Section

principle along with the GATS transparency provision in demanding more accountability from WTO Members that pursue rules restricting information flow without sufficient legal process.

3. <u>Reasonably, objectively and impartially administer rules</u>. Under the WTO, basic due process in regulation affecting trade is recognized not just as a matter of good governance, but an essential element of an efficient and well-functioning trading system. The GATS requires that WTO Members reasonably, objectively and impartially administer "measures of general application" affecting trade in services. This is no less true in online-related trade.

One of the key benefits of the WTO is promoting the "rule of law" in domestic economies and ensuring that governments regulate trade in a reasonable and objective manner. As the WTO Appellate Body stated in construing the comparable provision in the WTO agreement governing trade in goods (GATT, Article X), the rule established "certain minimum standards of due process, which encompass notions such as notice, transparency, fairness and equity."[47] One commentator has noted that "[t]he growing centrality of Article X [in WTO practice] reflects … an emerging global consensus regarding good governance values such as transparency, access to information, and participation."[48]

The particular GATS commitment (Article VI:1) provides that, in services sectors where a government has made specific pledges, "each Member shall ensure that all measures of general application affecting trade in services are administered in a reasonable, objective and impartial manner."

Governments have been found in violation of this obligation in the context of the parallel provision under the GATT.[49] The Dominican Republic was successfully challenged for unreasonably administering its tax regime – in that case, because it determined tax rates for a product (cigarettes) in an arbitrary manner without a basis in government rules in force. The WTO Panel noted that of the three methodologies contained in the law in force to determine the rate of consumption tax, the Dominican Republic chose none of them. There was no evidence that the Dominican Republic relied on any law in force at the time, nor evidence that it notified affected importers about its motivation to disregard retail selling prices as a basis for setting the rate.[50] Similarly, a WTO Panel rebuked Argentina for a enacting a regulation that gave domestic tanners access to sensitive business information regarding hide exporters, with whom the tanners did business. Divulging that kind of

---

I:2(D)), WT/L/432:2: "Review procedures shall include the opportunity for appeal, without penalty, by individuals or enterprises affected by any administrative action subject to review. If the initial right of appeal is to an administrative body, there shall in all cases be the opportunity to choose to appeal the decision to a judicial body. Notice of the decision on appeal shall be given to the appellant and the reasons for such decision shall be provided in writing. The appellant shall also be informed of any right to further appeal."

[47] *See* Panel Report, *European Communities – Customs*, ¶ 7.134, WT/DS315/R (June 16, 2006).

[48] Padideh Ala'i, *From the Periphery to the Center? The Evolving WTO Jurisprudence on Transparency and Good Governance*, in *Redesigning the World Trade Organization for the Twenty-First Century* 165, 166 (Debra P. Steger ed., 2009).

[49] GATT 1994 art. X:3(a). Only one case under the GATS has been decided by a dispute settlement panel that included this claim, and in that case, the complaining government did not sustain its burden of proof. *See* Panel Report, *United States – Gambling Services*, WT/DS285/R (Nov. 10, 2004); Appellate Body Report, *United States – Gambling Services*, WT/DS285/AB/R (Apr. 7, 2005).

[50] Panel Report, *Dominican Republic – Cigarettes*, ¶ 7.387, WT/DS302/R (May 19, 2005).

information was unreasonable, the Panel explained, because it did not serve the stated purpose of the regulation, which was to minimize fraud in the payment of export duties.[51]

In other cases, governments have been held to account for not administering measures of general application in a uniform manner.[52] For instance, a WTO panel and the Appellate Body agreed that the European Communities violated its WTO commitments by failing to uniformly administer its tariff classification system. The Panel noted "administration should be uniform in different places within a particular WTO Member." The EC was not permitted to maintain a "divergent tariff classification [that] has had and is likely to continue to have an adverse impact on the trading environment."[53]

Governments should insist on the reasonable, objective, and impartial administration of any limitations of the flow of online information that affect trade. The WTO should hold governments accountable for blocking Internet services in an inconsistent manner or without any basis in law.

4. <u>Maintain and promote non-discrimination</u>. Governments also use their censorship-related regimes in ways that disadvantage foreign firms instead of establishing the kinds of level playing fields envisioned in the WTO. This kind of discrimination is sometimes express – explicitly providing for less favorable treatment of foreign-sourced services or service suppliers – and sometimes *de facto* – imposing rules that appear even-handed on their face but disproportionately burden foreign-sourced services or service suppliers.

The GATS seeks to ensure a level playing field for local and foreign service providers and services. Regulations that disproportionately disadvantage businesses belonging to another WTO Member violate national treatment obligations assumed under GATS, provided that Member has included that services sector in its GATS schedule.

In particular, GATS Article XVII:1 provides for Members to operate by what is essentially the golden rule of trade. It holds that "each Member shall accord to services and service suppliers of any other Member, in respect of all measures affecting the supply of services, treatment no less favourable than that it accords to its own like services and service suppliers." "Less favourable" is further defined as "modif[ying] the conditions of competition in favour of services or service suppliers of the Member compared to like services or service suppliers of any other Member."[54]

This applies to Internet information regulation in two ways. First, when a government's regulations treat Internet traffic originating outside of the territory of that country less favorably than domestic traffic, there is a *prima facie* case of discrimination. Second, the WTO covers *de facto* discrimination, with the GATS explicitly prohibiting measures that modify the conditions of competition even if they appear to be "formally identical." In one well-known case, the WTO found discriminatory the European Union's system for allocating import

---

[51] Panel Report, *Argentina – Hides*, ¶¶ 11.90-11.94, WT/DS155/R (Feb. 16, 2001).
[52] *See* Panel Report, *European Communities – Customs*, ¶ 7.305, WT/DS315/R, (June 16, 2006); Panel Report, *European Communities – Bananas*, ¶¶ 7.211-7.212, WT/DS27/R/USA, (May 22, 1997).
[53] Panel Report, *European Communities – Customs*, ¶ 7.135, WT/DS315/R (June 16, 2006).
[54] GATS art. XVII:3.

quotas for bananas because of its effects on distributors from certain countries. This despite the fact that the EU policy on its face treated all imports the same, no matter the country of origin.[55]

Extending this into the realm of the Internet, the WTO could find a censorship law, rule or other measure to be discriminatory and favor local Internet services and service suppliers even if, on its face, the measure did not distinguish based on country of origin. In addition, WTO Members that favor local Internet services could also be violating the requirement that they ensure the impartial application of rules. (GATS VI:1)

5. Provide reasonable and non-discriminatory access to public telecommunications networks.

The mode and effect of many government restrictions on information flows is to restrict access of service providers to the telecommunications networks themselves, including through blocking of access, blocking of particular data transfers, or denial of licenses that enable a service provider to utilize the public telecommunications networks. Such actions run afoul of commitments made under the GATS Telecommunications Annex.

Specifically, WTO Members recognized the telecommunications networks serve as a "mode of transport" for the provision of services, and therefore negotiated an additional set of commitments to ensure that basic commitments made in particular service sectors were not undermined by restrictions on access to the telecommunications networks. In sectors where Members have made liberalization commitments, they are also required to afford foreign service suppliers reasonable and non-discriminatory access to their public telecommunications networks. (GATS Telecommunications Annex 5(a)). This obligation is further defined to include, among other obligations, that Members ensure foreign service suppliers may use the telecommunications networks to move information within and across borders, including to access information stored in offshore databases, with the limited exception for measures necessary to ensure the security and confidentiality of messages in a manner that is neither discriminatory nor a disguised restriction on trade. (GATS Telecommunications Annex 5(c) and (d)).

In addition, Members agreed that the only conditions that may be imposed on access to and use of the public telecommunications networks must be for the purpose of safeguarding the public service responsibilities of the network service providers and the technical integrity of the networks. (GATS Telecommunications Annex 5(3))

The GATS Telecommunications Annex has already been applied in WTO dispute settlement. Specifically, a WTO Panel ruled that where Mexico had made market access commitments with respect to various telecommunications services, it was not permitted to maintain measures that placed unreasonable restrictions on the access of foreign service

---

[55] *See* Appellate Body Report, *European Communities – Bananas*, ¶ 255, WT/DS27/AB/R (Sept. 9, 1997); Decision by the Arbitrators, *European Communities – Bananas* (Article 22.6), ¶ 5.94, WT/DS27/ARB (April 9, 1999), ("while any potential service supplier originating in third countries is not *de iure* precluded from acquiring "newcomer" status, in our view, the criteria for demonstrating the requisite expertise in order to qualify as an importer of bananas as "newcomer" create in their overall impact less favourable conditions of competition for service suppliers of the United States or other Members than for like service suppliers of EC origin").

suppliers to the public telecommunications networks in order to provide these services.[56] Thus, where Members' actions have the effect of denying foreign service suppliers in covered sectors reasonable access to the public telecommunications networks, and in particular where the effect is to disrupt cross-border information flows, they can be held to account under the GATS Telecommunications Annex.

6. <u>Provide for fair market access</u>. GATS prohibits WTO Members from restricting the number of foreign suppliers in service sectors where they have made market access commitments; this includes using measures that effectively create a so-called "zero-quota."[57] Such measures would include both technical blocking measures and other regulatory prohibitions making it impossible to provide or access particular types of services. Censorship-related measures that block entire Internet services in scheduled sectors violate obligations outlined in Article XVI of GATS.

The GATS market access obligation, however, is limited to measures that impose specific types of market access restrictions -- namely, limitations on the number of suppliers, the value of services transactions, number of service operations or total quantity of service output, number of employees, type of legal entity, or participation of foreign capital. As a result, the market access provisions of the GATS may not always be useful in addressing measures that degrade the quality of the market access afforded to some services or service suppliers. This limitation in the GATS provision makes it all the more important that governments pursue new disciplines to favor the free flow of information (see Section V).

Exceptional measures must be narrowly tailored

Despite these rules, there is no doubt that WTO Members will continue to take actions to restrict the flow of information that are inconsistent with their previous pledges on transparency, administration of rules, non-discrimination and market access. In the case of a challenge to their information regulation practices, they would likely try to invoke one of the "general exceptions" in the GATS. It would be up to other Members to ensure that the exceptions do not become the rule. Their challenge would be clear: protect Members' right to pursue legitimate policy goals while preventing the broad application of exceptions from weakening national commitments under GATS.

In the area of Internet information regulation, governments would most likely seek to justify their actions as necessary either to "protect public morals" or to "maintain public order". But these exceptions require that a government meet three primary requirements, which are provided for in the GATS (Article XIV).

First, a government must show that its measure is necessary to achieve the stated objective. Among other things, the Member state must prove that there is no "reasonably available," less trade-restrictive alternative to protect public morals or maintain public order.[58] The so-called "necessity test" is not easy to meet and is not judged simply by whether a government itself considers that the restriction is necessary to meet its objective. In fact, many governments in different contexts have failed to provide objective evidence that would meet the criteria and have therefore been unable to

---

[56] FN -- Mexico-Measures Affecting Telecommunications Services, WT/DS204/R (April 2004))
[57] Appellate Body Report, *United States – Gambling Services*, ¶¶ 214-238, WT/DS285/AB/R (Apr. 7, 2005).
[58] Appellate Body Report, *United States – Gambling Services*, ¶ 304, WT/DS285/AB/R (Apr. 7, 2005).

justify actions inconsistent with WTO rules. China, for example, failed to convince the Appellate Body that certain publication restrictions were "apt to make a material contribution to the protection of public morals."[59]

A government may be able to show *some* nexus between particular government information regulation and the maintenance of public order or protection of public morals. However, governments regularly overreach in their approach to Internet restrictions. In so doing, those governments violate their GATS commitment and must then pursue the least trade-disruptive, reasonably available measure.

For example, in the recent *China – Audiovisual* case, China had established a censorship mechanism under which only designated entities were authorized to import media and entertainment products. These entities were also responsible for reviewing the imported content. The Appellate Body ruled that even if this discriminatory import of media and entertainment were proven to help protect public morals, it could not be deemed "necessary" under the relevant WTO exception because less restrictive and equally effective alternatives were reasonably available. The Chinese government could, for example, have reviewed imported content itself, thereby imposing a lesser burden on content providers while achieving the same objective.[60]

Similarly, in the *Korea – Beef* case, although the Appellate Body acknowledged that the establishment of a separate sales channel for imported beef supported Korea's legitimate objective of reducing fraud, that measure was not the least restrictive method of achieving this objective. The government could have achieved its desired policy goals through ordinary policing measures. As a result, Korea was not permitted to invoke a "necessity" exception to its trade commitments.[61]

This kind of challenge could arise when a government orders Internet access providers to block entire websites or services on the basis that some content violates local regulations said to be necessary to protect public morals – *e.g.*, some user postings on the website consist of hate speech. In this case, the order could be challenged on the basis of non-objective and unreasonable administration of laws, a violation of transparency obligations, or discrimination, depending on the facts. In that scenario, a government would likely seek to justify the *prima facie* violation under the general exceptions, but it would be unlikely to succeed: there are reasonably available alternatives that would address its legitimate objective and restrict trade less than a full blockage.

In the case of Internet censorship, a reasonably available and less trade-disruptive alternative to blocking an entire online service is to, for example, ask the service provider to take down the specific material deemed offensive. If the service provider complies, the issue would be resolved without interfering with the operation of the web service or the harming businesses and individuals that rely on the web service. Alternatively, the government could direct the provider to block only those web pages reachable via youtube.com that contain the offensive content.

Second, the GATS imposes an additional limitation on cases in which governments attempt to justify a trade restriction based on "public order." The GATS specifically provides that a government may only invoke the public order exception "where a genuine and sufficiently serious threat is posed to

---

[59] Appellate Body Report, *China – Publications and Audiovisual Products*, ¶¶ 289-297, WT/DS363/AB/R (Dec. 21, 2009).
[60] *Ibid.*
[61] Appellate Body Report, *Korea – Beef*, ¶¶ 158-182, WT/DS161/AB/R (Dec. 11, 2000).

one of the fundamental interests of society."[62] The negotiators who concluded the WTO were evidently particularly concerned that governments would abuse the public order exception.

Third, even if a government could justify an Internet restrictive measure as "necessary" to protect public order or morals, it would still have to demonstrate that the measure was applied without prejudice. GATS Article XIV requires that any Member seeking to justify a WTO inconsistency must not apply that measure "in a manner which would constitute a means of arbitrary or unjustifiable discrimination between countries where like conditions prevail, or is a disguised restriction on trade in services." The WTO would likely reject exceptions that discriminate among trading partners or disguise trade restrictions.

---

[62] GATS art. XIV, n.5.

www.ingramcontent.com/pod-product-compliance
Lightning Source LLC
Chambersburg PA
CBHW052029280526
45793CB00005B/1180